D0578877

10360

4 Apr 88
$10.90

Millard, Anne
Egypt, 3118 BC-AD 642

DATE DUE			
SEP 27			
OCT 22			
NOV MAR 3 1			
FEB 2 9			
FEB -8			
FEB 2			
60 DE			

EGYPT

© Aladdin Books Ltd 1987

Designed and produced by
Aladdin Books Ltd
70 Old Compton Street
London W1

First published in the
United States in 1988 by
Franklin Watts
387 Park Avenue South
New York, NY 10016

Design   David West
              Children's Book Design

Editor   Denny Robson

Researcher Cecilia Weston-Baker

Illustrator Rob Shone

Consultant George Hart,
              Education Office,
              British Museum, London.

ISBN 0-531-10537-7

Library of Congress Catalog
Card Number: 87-51286

Printed in Belgium

CONTENTS

GREAT CIVILIZATIONS

EGYPT
3118BC – AD642

Anne Millard

FRANKLIN WATTS
New York · London · Toronto · Sydney

INTRODUCTION

The civilization of Egypt is one of the oldest and greatest in the world. We are lucky that so much material from the time of the ancient Egyptians has survived for us to study. We can admire the remains of their huge buildings and get to know individuals from their statues. We can discover details of their daily lives from the paintings in their tombs. From the writings which survive we can learn about what they thought, felt and did. The ancient Egyptians believed that death was just a door to another, eternal life and that they could take all they would need there by putting it in their tombs. Because of this we can handle objects, clothes and furniture that were in daily use thousands of years ago.

Egyptian civilization developed on the banks of the Nile. Herodotus, a clever Greek historian, wrote that Egypt was "the gift of the Nile." Egypt is an area almost entirely without rain and most of the land is stark desert. Every year, heavy rains in the south send water into the Nile. Before the building of modern dams, this caused the Nile to overflow its banks. This was the Inundation, a flood which brought with it rich, fertile mud to renew the soil.

This book divides the story of ancient Egypt into four periods: the unification and the pyramid age; the middle kingdom and its collapse; the empire at its height; and finally the decline of ancient Egypt.

As Egypt was flooded for several weeks every year, the river was the easiest way to move all heavy loads. But water wasn't the only gift of the Nile. Its waters teemed with fish. Reed beds supplied papyrus, used to make a kind of paper, and reeds for building and making a variety of goods from pens to sandals. The reed thickets were also home to many kinds of birds and hippopotami which were hunted by the nobles.

UNIFICATION OF EGYPT c3118-2181 BC

Egypt's first villages of farmers gradually united until they formed two states — Upper Egypt in the south (the Valley), with its capital at Hierakonpolis where the kings wore the White Crown, and Lower Egypt in the north (the Delta), with its capital at Buto and the Red Crown for its kings. Then a king of Upper Egypt called Menes conquered the north, uniting the two lands for the first time. He built a new capital at Memphis and he and his successors erected the rectangular mudbrick tombs called *mastabas* at nearby Sakkara.

The period which modern scholars call the Old Kingdom was one of the greatest in Egypt's long history. Egypt traded widely and amassed riches. Texts were written on all manner of topics and tomb goods reveal the skills of the craftsmen and the elegant taste of the people.

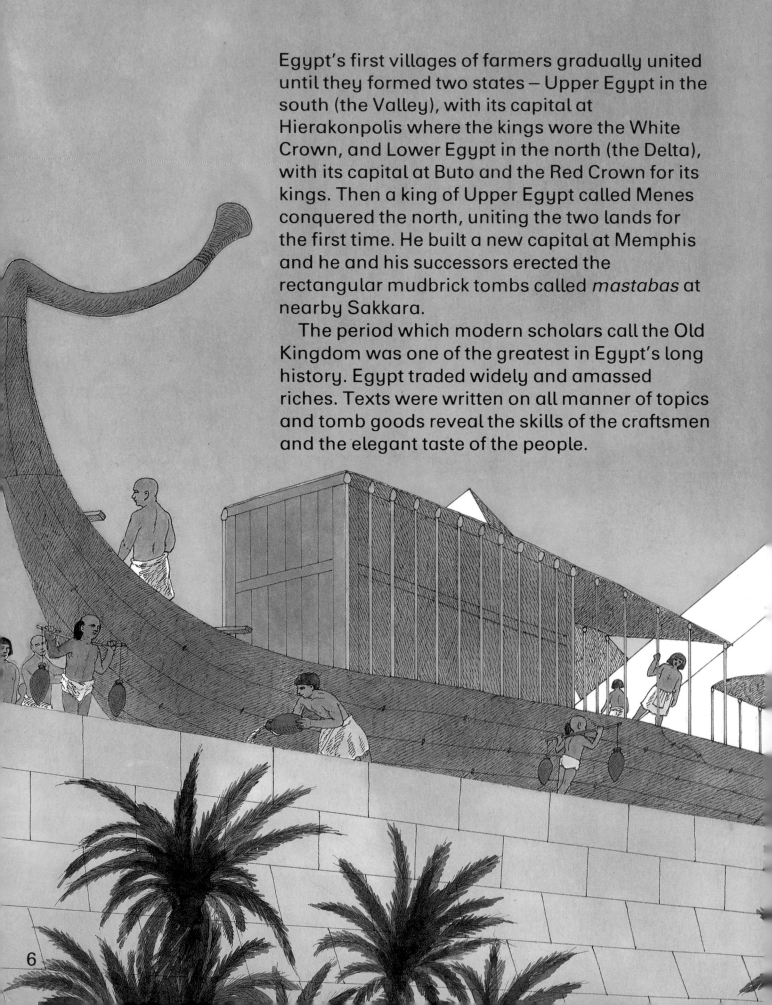

King Khufu of the 4th Dynasty built his pyramid at Giza. It is the largest of all the pyramids. Its temples were to provide all he needed in the next world. Among the things he would need were boats to travel in, so real boats were buried in pits around the pyramid. One has been found and restored to its former glory.

MEDITERRANEAN SEA

Buto

Trade with Middle East

LOWER EGYPT

Giza ▲
Sakkara ▲
The Fayum
Memphis

RED SEA

Herakleopolis

Nile

Abydos

Hierakonpolis
First cataract

UPPER EGYPT

Aswan
Border of Egypt in early Dynastic period

Trade and raiding

NUBIA

Second cataract

Fertile area

Datechart

THE UNIFICATION

c3118 BC Menes, King of Upper Egypt, conquers Lower Egypt and unites the two lands.

THE ARCHAIC PERIOD

c3100-2686 BC 1st and 2nd Dynasties. Monuments are built of mud bricks.

THE OLD KINGDOM

c2686-2613 BC 3rd Dynasty. The architect Imhotep (later worshipped as a god) builds the Step Pyramid at Sakkara for King Zoser. The pyramid of the later King Huni is turned from a step to a straight-sided pyramid.

c2613-2494 BC 4th Dynasty. The famous Giza group of pyramids is built. Mining expeditions to Sinai. Regular trade with Byblos and Nubia.

c2494-2345 BC 5th Dynasty. Kings devoted to the sun god Re and take the title "Son of Re." First known trip to Punt. The pyramids are built at Abusir.

c2345-2181 BC 6th Dynasty. Canal cut in First Cataract (place where rocks fill the river and block it to shipping) to speed journeys to Nubia. More power for district governors called nomarchs, so royal power and prestige are reduced. Pepi II reigns 94 years.

The pyramids

In the 3rd Dynasty Egypt was wealthy. As craftsmen were using stone with great skill, it was decided to build the king's tomb in stone so that it would last forever. The architect in charge was called Imhotep. He designed a new style of tomb – a pyramid of steps so the dead king could climb up to the sky to become one of the eternal stars.

Later it was decided to have pyramids with straight sides, but the first one was a failure. The angle of the sides was too steep and had to be altered making the "Bent" pyramid.

To provide the king with all the things he would need in the next world, a great complex of buildings was put up around his pyramid. His courtiers were buried near by in *mastaba* tombs.

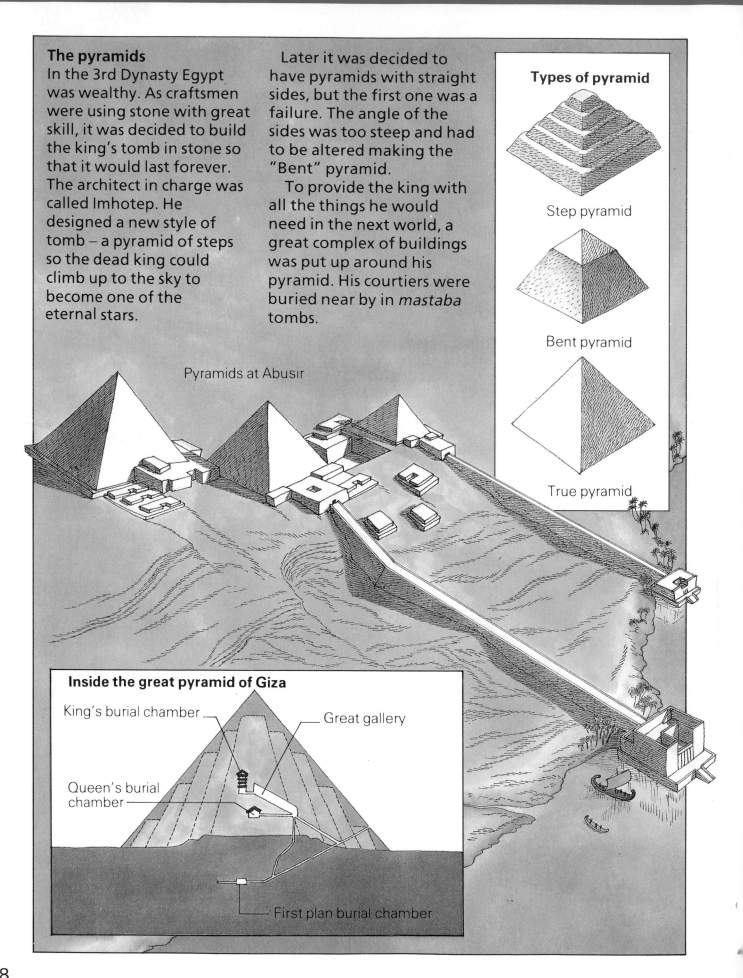

Types of pyramid

Step pyramid

Bent pyramid

True pyramid

Pyramids at Abusir

Inside the great pyramid of Giza

King's burial chamber

Great gallery

Queen's burial chamber

First plan burial chamber

The pharaoh

For the Egyptians, their king the pharaoh was more than just a powerful man. When he was wearing his Double Crown, seated on his throne and carrying his Crook and Flail, the spirit of the god Horus entered him and he became a god. It was also thought that he was descended from the sun god Re. In order to keep this special, divine blood pure, it was the custom for the king to marry his sister.

Many of the pharaohs were warriors. Our illustration shows the first king Menes executing his northern rival.

White crown of Upper Egypt   Red crown of Lower Egypt   Double crown

Life at the royal court

The king was the source of all power and wealth. Life at court revolved around him, with priests and servants to care for and entertain him.

Being a god set apart from ordinary mortals, the king had a vizier to see that his policies and orders were carried out by the many officials he had appointed to act for him.

Because he was so holy, he was a remote figure, held in great awe. But texts suggest that some kings liked to relax with music and dancing, storytelling and magicians.

A nobleman's estate
Most Egyptians lived in small houses but the rich had large estates like the one in the picture. The villas were set in cool, shady gardens with high walls for privacy.

Behind the villa were the servants' quarters, stables for the horses and stalls for the cattle being fattened for the table. Pigeons and other birds were kept in an aviary and also eaten.

An estate like this would produce most of the things needed by the owner, so there were also workshops where weavers, carpenters, metalworkers and other craftsmen could work.

A farmer's house

This is the home of a peasant farmer. Like the nobleman's house it is made of mud bricks baked hard by the sun. It has only three or four rooms but the cooking and many household tasks are done in the open air. The family can relax on the roof, shaded by the awning and in the breeze.

Granaries and supplies are kept in the courtyard where the farm animals are guarded at night.

The farmer's year

In October when the water of the Inundation went down, farmers plowed their lands with oxen and wooden plows. Others walked behind scattering seed which was trodden in by flocks of sheep. As crops grew, tax men came around and worked out how much should be paid as tax.

Harvest came in March and April. Sickles were used to cut the ears of grain which were loaded into baskets and taken on donkeys to the threshing floor. Here the grain was separated from the ears and winnowed to remove the chaff. It was then taken to be stored in granaries under the watchful eyes of scribes.

Water from the Inundation was stored in canals and guided into the fields through small ditches. In the New Kingdom the *shaduf* was invented to lift water from a canal to a higher one. This simple device is still in use today, as the photograph shows, but it is now being replaced by electrically driven pumps.

MIDDLE KINGDOM AND AFTER

When the Old Kingdom collapsed an unhappy time followed with civil wars, rival claimants to the throne, disorder, foreign invasions and famine. At last the ruler of Thebes, Mentuhotep, swept north and reunited the two lands again.

Under his wise rule Egypt recovered from the recent troubles, but his family was later replaced by that of a high official called Amenemhat. He founded the 12th Dynasty and it was under this that Egypt enjoyed another of the great periods in its history. Egypt was well run. In the Fayum rich farm land was created by partly draining the large lake there. Trade flourished bringing more wealth. Arts and crafts bloomed and some of Egypt's most famous stories were written. Many of Egypt's eastern neighbors were much influenced by its culture, while its armies marched south and conquered Nubia.

As the king was also a god it was a terrible crime to harm him. But the unfortunate King Amenemhat 1 was attacked and murdered by members of his household. His son and chosen heir Senusret, who had been crowned in his father's lifetime, outwitted the villains and saved his throne.

c2181-1567 BC

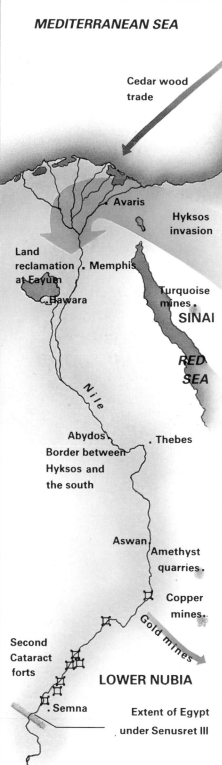

MEDITERRANEAN SEA

Byblos

Cedar wood trade

Avaris

Hyksos invasion

Land reclamation at Fayum

Memphis

Hawara

Turquoise mines

SINAI

RED SEA

Nile

Abydos
Border between Hyksos and the south

Thebes

Aswan

Amethyst quarries

Copper mines

Gold mines

Second Cataract forts

LOWER NUBIA

Semna

Extent of Egypt under Senusret III

THE MIDDLE KINGDOM
c2133-1991 BC 11th Dynasty. A rival line of kings had ruled in Thebes for several years. In 2040 BC Mentuhotep II overthrows 10th Dynasty kings and unites Egypt.

1991-1786 BC 12th Dynasty. Amenemhat I founds new line of kings. Their pyramids are built around the entrance to the Fayum. Nubia conquered and forts built on Second Cataract.

1897-1878 BC Senusret II begins work to reclaim land in the Fayum.

1878-1843 BC Senusret III, great warrior king, crushes Nubian resistance.

1789-1786 BC As there is no male heir, Princess Sobekneferu rules as "king."

1786-1633 BC 13th Dynasty. People from over the Eastern frontier come into Egypt and conquer most of the land.

2ND INTERMEDIATE PERIOD
1633-1567 BC Egypt ruled by the Hyksos.

Datechart
1ST INTERMEDIATE PERIOD
c2181-2160 BC 7th and 8th Dynasties.

c2160-2040 BC 9th and 10th Dynasties set up by princes of Herakleopolis.

13

Scribes and scrolls

The government of Egypt was based on keeping records. Every order, action, payment and deal had to be recorded. As many Egyptians could not write, scribes often hired out their services to clients. People kept all the family records in case they were ever needed – in a court case, for example.

A scribe might take notes on bits of broken pottery but a finished piece of work was written on a long scroll of papyrus. To work, a scribe sat cross-legged on the floor with his scroll resting on a writing board. He used reed pens dipped in water and he made his own paints from various mineral substances.

Making papyrus

The diagram below shows the different stages involved in making papyrus. (1) Peel off green outer case of the papyrus stem. (2) Split white inner core of stem into thin strips then soak them in clean water. (3) Form a page by overlapping strips of papyrus. (4) Hammer page to get the strips to stick together. (5) Smooth surface.

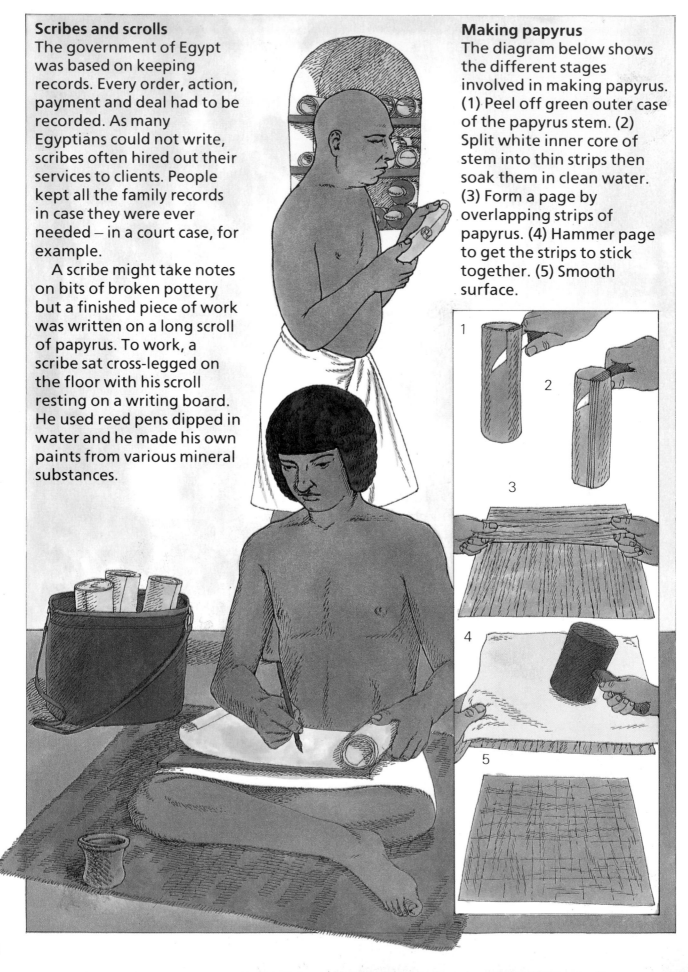

1
2
3
4
5

Hieroglyphs

Hieroglyphs, a form of picture writing, appeared in Egypt shortly before the Unification. Some signs represent one letter, some 2,3,4 or 5 letters and yet others actual objects. No punctuation was used. All letters are consonants. The Egyptians did not write down vowels. We have to guess how words sounded with the help of Coptic, ancient Egyptian's descendent, now only used in the Egyptian Christian Church. There were also two scripts for daily use – Hieratic and Demotic.

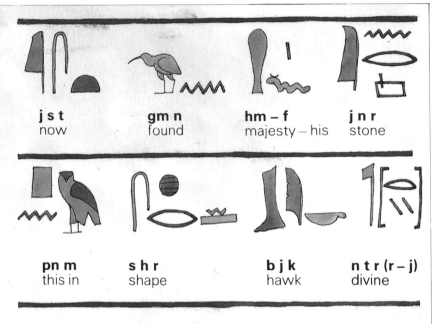

j s t
now

g m n
found

h m – f
majesty – his

j n r
stone

p n m
this in

s h r
shape

b j k
hawk

n t r (r – j)
divine

Translation: His majesty found this stone in the shape of a divine hawk.

Education

Those who could afford it sent their sons to school when the child was about five years old. Girls did not go to school.

First a child had to learn to write. This was done by endlessly copying texts. The more advanced pupils then had to master all the other subjects they would need.

Fun and games

A wide variety of toys like those in the photograph have been found including dolls, tops, balls, models and figures with moving parts. Children and adults enjoyed games played on boards with counters and for the energetic there were many exciting team games.

The army

As in the Old Kingdom, the army of the Middle Kingdom was made up entirely of foot soldiers. They were armed with spears, swords, maces, axes and bows and arrows. As a protection they carried shields but had no armor. The king had a bodyguard and there was a small army of trained, professional soldiers. But when more men were needed for a campaign, officials went out and conscripted men to serve in the army as recruits. It was part of the labor tax all men owed the king.

Egypt's wealth

Papyrus, food, wine, and jewels, like those on the left, were traded for the materials Egypt lacked and for luxuries. Trading was organized by the government.

Byblos (in modern Lebanon) supplied Egypt with timber from its great cedar forests as well as wine, silver, slaves and other goods. Copper and turquoise were mined in Sinai.

Nubia was the source of many of Egypt's slaves and much of its gold, copper and amethyst. Goods from further south — ebony, ivory, ostrich plumes and panther skins — also reached Egypt through Nubia.

In the Middle Kingdom Egypt conquered Nubia. To protect the new frontier, fortresses were built around the Second Cataract. Our picture shows a caravan of trade goods arriving.

The Hyksos invasion

It was the Egyptians' custom to allow nomads from across their eastern frontier to come into the Delta to pasture their flocks. In the 13th Dynasty, Egypt ran into trouble. Disputes over the throne had badly weakened the government. Without strict frontier controls more easterners came in. Finally, using horses and chariots which were not known in Egypt, they conquered most of the land.

These invaders are known as Hyksos, meaning "desert chieftains." At last the princes of Thebes rallied and drove them out.

17

EMPIRE AT ITS HEIGHT 1567-1085 BC

In the New Kingdom, Egypt was at the height of its power. Having chased the Hyksos out, Egypt went on to conquer a vast empire. The army was enlarged and its soldiers were mostly full-time professionals. Body armor and new weapons were introduced. A chariot squadron was formed which was often led by the king himself.

Egypt's influence was extended from the 4th Cataract of the Nile in the south to the Euphrates River in the east. Nubia and Kush completely adopted Egyptian ways but some of the eastern vassals rebelled against Egyptian rule. In this they were helped by Egypt's great rivals, the Mitanni and the Hittites.

In the reign of Akhenaten the Egyptians lost many of their eastern possessions. Seti I and Ramesses II fought to regain the lost lands but did not succeed in getting them all back.

18

Incense was vital to the Egyptians. They needed it for temple services and burying their dead. They made long, difficult voyages to Punt (probably in modern Somaliland) to buy incense. In the 18th Dynasty Queen Hatshepsut sent an expedition to buy incense trees so they could be grown in Egypt. The picture shows her officials meeting the Chief of Punt and his wife. They returned home in triumph with incense, trees and other valuable goods.

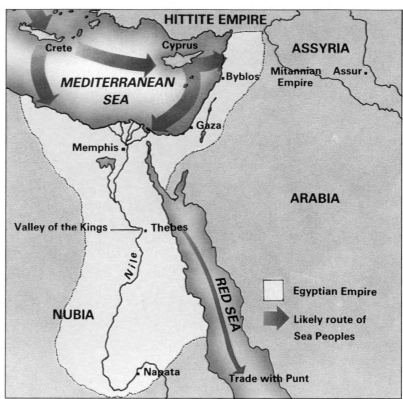

Datechart
NEW KINGDOM
1567-1320 BC 18th Dynasty. Hyksos driven out. Conquest of the empire.

1546-1525 BC The reign of Amenhotep I. He sets up a community of workmen to build the royal tombs.

1526-1512 BC Tuthmosis I has the first tomb cut in the Valley of the Kings.

1503-1482 BC Queen Hatshepsut seizes the throne and rules as king.

1504-1450 BC Tuthmosis III, greatest of Egypt's warrior pharaohs.

1417-1379 BC Empire at its height under King Amenhotep III.

1379-1362 BC Akhenaten – the "heretic" pharaoh. Capital at Amarna where he worships one god but neglects the empire, losing many eastern provinces.

1361-1352 BC Tutankhamun restores old gods.

1348-1320 BC Horemheb reorganizes Egypt.

1320-1200 BC 19th Dynasty. Seti I and Ramesses II win back some of the Eastern empire. Abu Simbel temple built. The Dynasty ends with struggles over the throne.

1200-1085 BC 20th Dynasty. Ramesses III saves Egypt from the Sea Peoples. A period of decline follows.

Egypt at war

When Egypt conquered its empire the fighting was all on land. Ships were used for transport only to speed the army to trouble spots and to spare it tiring marches.

But in the 20th Dynasty Egypt itself was attacked. The enemy was the Sea Peoples. They came from the northeast Mediterranean and were seeking new homes.

They burned many cities and destroyed the Hittite empire. Ramesses III waited at his frontier. He defeated them only after desperate battles on land and sea and so saved Egypt.

Tribute and trade

Once conquered, people had to send tribute to Egypt to prove their loyalty, but they could also continue trading with Egypt. Defeated princes had to send their sons to Egypt as hostages to be brought up as loyal vassals. Foreign princesses were sent to be minor wives of the pharaohs.

The gold mines of Nubia were worked so effectively that one king wrote to the pharaoh asking for gold as in Egypt it was as common as dust! Egyptians became fabulously wealthy. They used their riches to adorn their temples, palaces, houses and bodies and to fill their tombs with treasures.

Gods and temples

The Egyptians worshipped many gods and goddesses. The favorites in the New Kingdom were Amun, King of the gods, Osiris, god of the dead, his loving wife Isis and their son Horus, and Hathor, goddess of love and beauty. To persuade them to visit earth, the Egyptians built splendid temples like the one at Abu Simbel, shown in the photograph.

| Montu | Amun | Thoth | Khnum | Horus | Sakhmet | Sobek | Anubis | Isis | Osiris | Hathor |

Akhenaten and Nefertiti

King Amenhotep IV felt such special devotion to the god Aten (who appeared as the sun's disk) that he changed his name to Akhenaten. He and his wife Nefertiti went to live in a new city, built for Aten's glory. He ordered that no other god was to be worshipped. Akhenaten was so busy with his god that he neglected the empire and so lost many cities to the Hittites. Later generations cursed him as that "heretic" and his god and his city were abandoned.

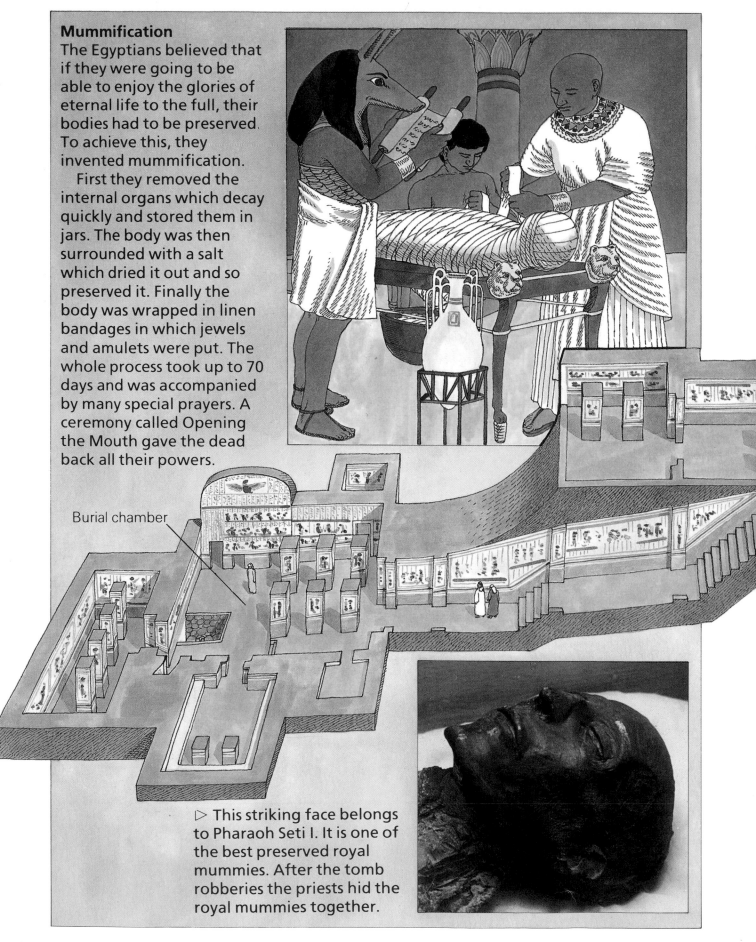

Mummification

The Egyptians believed that if they were going to be able to enjoy the glories of eternal life to the full, their bodies had to be preserved. To achieve this, they invented mummification.

First they removed the internal organs which decay quickly and stored them in jars. The body was then surrounded with a salt which dried it out and so preserved it. Finally the body was wrapped in linen bandages in which jewels and amulets were put. The whole process took up to 70 days and was accompanied by many special prayers. A ceremony called Opening the Mouth gave the dead back all their powers.

Burial chamber

▷ This striking face belongs to Pharaoh Seti I. It is one of the best preserved royal mummies. After the tomb robberies the priests hid the royal mummies together.

The Valley of the Kings

The kings saw that even pyramids provided no real protection against robbers. So in the New Kingdom tombs were cut deep into the sides of a valley on the West Bank at Thebes. This is the famous Valley of the Kings. Members of the royal family also had rock cut tombs in the Valley of the Queens. But the robbers still looted all except Tutankhamun's tomb.

The largest tomb in the Valley of the Kings belonged to Seti I. It is decorated with scenes showing how the king would triumph in the Next World.

Tomb of Seti I

The village of the workmen

The valley now called Deir el Medinah was the home of the workmen who cut and decorated tombs for the royal family and the nobles. A special village, shown in the illustration on the left, was built for them in the desert so they could be near their work. They were well paid by the State for this important work. Other craftsmen who made the objects to go in the tombs, like the goldsmiths above, worked in special workshops attached to the palaces and temples.

FOREIGN PHARAOHS 1085 BC-AD 642

One of the worst disasters ever to hit Egypt occurred when it was overrun by the Assyrians, who were cruel and ruthless. When angered by Egypt's Nubian kings and their supporters, the Assyrians sacked Thebes. The city never recovered from its losses despite the loyal efforts of its citizens.

After the triumphs of Ramesses III against the Sea Peoples, Egypt entered into a long period of slow decline. The empire in the east was lost and later Nubia broke away to form a separate kingdom under its own princes. In Egypt officials often became lazy or dishonest and the government was badly run. Robbers looted the royal tombs. Egypt still had wealth, but the power and the glory were gone.

Then rival kings began to struggle for power and, as had happened before under similar circumstances, Egypt fell victim to foreign invaders. First a line of Libyan kings ruled, then Nubians, Assyrians and later Persians. Only during the glorious 26th Dynasty did Egypt have full independence for any length of time and even then several of the kings hired Greek soldiers and allowed Greek merchants to settle.

MACEDONIA

Samothrace

Lesbos

Athens

Sparta

Samos

Thera

Crete

Cyprus

Byblos

MEDITERRANEAN SEA

Jerusalem

Gaza

Alexandria

Saïs

Tanis

Bubastis

Cyrenaica

Memphis

Nile

RED SEA

Thebes

☐ Ptolemaic Empire at its height

Datechart

3RD INTERMEDIATE PERIOD

1085-945 BC 21st Dynasty. Kings rule from Tanis in the Delta but High Priests of Amun rule the south from Thebes.

945-715 BC 22nd Dynasty. A Libyan family rules from Bubastis.

818-715 BC 23rd and 24th Dynasties overlap with end of 22nd.

728 BC Piankhy, king of Nubia, invades Egypt and founds the 25th Dynasty.

663 BC Sack of Thebes.

LATE PERIOD

664-525 BC 26th Dynasty rules from Saïs.

525-404 BC Rule of Persians as 27th Dynasty.

404-341 BC 28th to 30th Dynasties of native kings.

341-332 BC Return of the Persians.

332 BC Conquest of Egypt by Alexander the Great.

323 BC Death of Alexander.

323-30 BC The Ptolemies rule Egypt.

30 BC Egypt conquered by Rome.

1st century AD Arrival of Christianity in Egypt.

AD 639-642 Conquest by the Arabs. Introduction of Islam.

25

The royal cities

From 1085 BC the capital was moved as each dynasty rose and fell. First Tanis was favored, then Bubastis and later Saïs. Memphis was also an important center. Even in decline Egypt was still rich and the temples at these cities were magnificent.

Tanis was the capital during the 21st Dynasty. The kings were buried within the Amun temple enclosure with their jewels and vessels of gold and silver. In Thebes the High Priests of Amun ruled and some even took royal titles.

One of the most popular goddesses of the period was Bast. She appeared to her faithful worshippers as a cat (shown in the picture below). She represented the life-giving warmth of the sun but when angered she punished offenders. Her home was in Bubastis.

Magic and medicine

Egyptian doctors were highly respected. A few texts on medicine have survived and we can see that doctors were well-informed and efficient. Because Egyptians were a religious people, every medicine and treatment had to be accompanied by prayers. Doctors realized there were many diseases they could not cure and for those they used magic potions and spells. Magic played an important role in their lives and they used charms to protect and bring good luck.

Mathematics and building

The Rhind Papyrus (photograph right) shows ancient calculations about triangles and pyramids. Such documents indicate that the Egyptians used their mathematical skills in many practical ways.

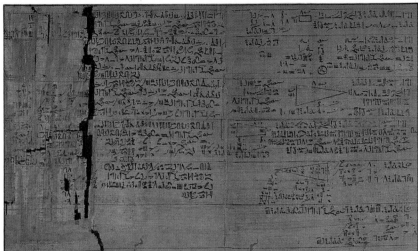

Mathematics was applied to temple building, for example (shown right). A layer of stone was put in place, the areas between were filled with sand and a short ramp was built. A new layer of stones was dragged into place, and so on until the roof was on.

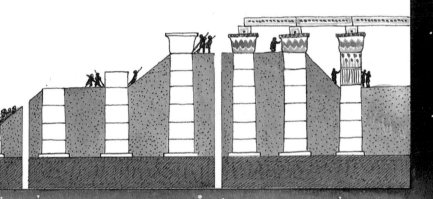

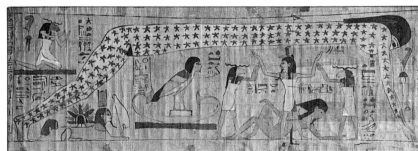

Astronomy

Egyptian priests made a special study of the stars and planets. This enabled them to invent a calendar of 365 days. There were 12 months of 30 days each with five extra days as holy feasts. Each week had 10 days, all with their own star groups. Each day had 24 hours.

The papyrus shown above illustrates one ancient Egyptian story about how the world was made by the creator god, Atum. His two children were Shu (air) and Tefnut (moisture). They too had children – Geb (earth) and Nut (sky). Shu held up Nut so her body arched over Geb her husband. The stars were their children.

The Nubian conquerors

The Egyptians and Nubians who ruled Nubia after it had broken away from Egypt held on to their Egyptian ways, particularly their devotion to the god Amun. This picture shows Amun in his ram form with one of the Nubian kings. King Piankhy claimed that Amun had sent him to invade Egypt and restore his worship to its old, pure form.

He and his successors did much to try and revive the greatness of former days. But they angered the Assyrians who took violent revenge. The Nubians fled home once more where they continued to rule.

Alexandria and the Ptolemies

Many Egyptians resented the Persians' rule. Some set themselves up as kings, but the Persians regained control. When Alexander arrived in Egypt during his conquest of the Persian empire, he was hailed as a deliverer and accepted as a true pharaoh. This photograph shows a statue of Alexander as pharaoh.

While in Egypt, Alexander ordered a great city to be built on the coast — Alexandria. The painting shows how it might have looked at this time. It became Egypt's new capital with good harbors and a great lighthouse. It had a theater, a library and a museum. As a center of learning the city was famous throughout the Mediterranean world.

When Alexander died his empire broke up as his generals struggled for power. Ptolemy took over Egypt and founded a new dynasty named after him. In many ways the Ptolemies were a remarkable family and produced some very able rulers. Unfortunately their family feuds were fierce and violent and paved the way for Rome to interfere.

Egypt under Rome

The last ruler of an independent Egypt was Queen Cleopatra. Because of her love for a Roman general, Mark Antony, she became involved in the bitter civil wars which tore Rome apart after the murder of her earlier protector, Julius Caesar. When defeated by Octavian she chose to kill herself. Tradition says she used a venomous snake.

Egypt became just another province of the Roman empire. It was important, however, as its grain was used to feed Rome's hordes of poor citizens. Christianity arrived early in Egypt. It had its saints and martyrs and the first monasteries were set up there. Later when the new Rome was built at Constantinople, Egypt was ruled as part of the Eastern or Byzantine empire until the Arab conquest.

When the Greeks began to visit Egypt they were greatly impressed by its learning, its religion and its monuments. Through the Greeks and the Romans some of Egypt's ancient wisdom has been passed down to us.

The modern world also respects Egypt's ancient culture. Universities study it and archeologists dig there. When the building of the Aswan Dam threatened the monuments in Nubia, countries all over the world helped to mount a massive rescue operation to save them. Thousands of tourists visit Egypt drawn by the grandeur of the ancient civilization. And there is still much to find. New secrets and new objects are being discovered each year.

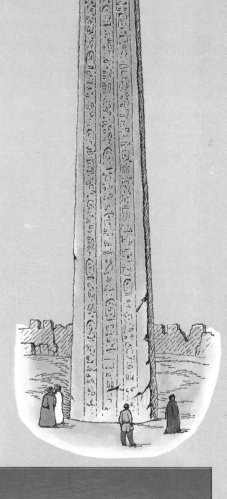

Egyptian treasure
The most famous find of all time was the tomb of the boy king Tutankhamun in 1922. It had been overlooked by the tomb robbers and so still contained his fabulous treasures. The photograph shows the king's death mask.

Egyptian monuments
Obelisks, like the one on the right, were emblems of the sun god and once stood in pairs at temple gates. But few remain in Egypt. They were taken last century to capitals all over the world. But pyramids cannot be moved. They stand like monuments to eternity.

The Nile today

First the British and then the Egyptian governments built dams at Aswan in order to control the waters of the Nile. The modern High Dam at Aswan also provides Egypt with hydro-electric power. But the Nile is still also Egypt's highway. Working barges chug past as tourists drift along and the local ferries pass back and forth as they did in ancient times.

The Rosetta Stone

The meaning of hieroglyphs was lost until the discovery of the Rosetta Stone. It provided the clue that scholars needed to help them decipher the ancient texts. The text of the Rosetta Stone is written three times – in Greek, hieroglyphs and demotic. By using the Greek letters and matching them to the pictures, scholars solved the ancient mystery.

INDEX

Photographic Credits:
Page II: Hutchison Library; page 15:
Michael Holford; page 21: Greg Evans
Library; page 22: George Hart; page 27
(both): Robert Harding Library; page 28:
Ancient Art and Architecture; pages 30 and
31: Zefa; page 30: Tony Stone Associates.

PRINTED IN BELGIUM BY
proost
INTERNATIONAL BOOK PRODUCTION